The $100K Crash: Lessons from the Entrepreneur Test Dummy

David A. Greene Jr.

FOREWORD

Embarking on entrepreneurship as a 40+ year-old Black man in America has been a road filled with triumphs, trials, and profound lessons. It's a journey that has shaped and tested me, deepening my understanding of what it takes to build something meaningful. In *The $100K Crash: Lessons from the Entrepreneur Test Dummy*, I lay bare the raw truth about my personal path—a path that began with high hopes, took sharp detours, and led me to invaluable insights.

This book isn't just about financial loss; it's about resilience and growth when facing failure head-on. My hope is that my story resonates, inspires, and equips you to avoid the same missteps. I'm sharing lessons not to dwell on regrets, but to pave a smoother road for the next entrepreneur.

Faith and purpose are the foundation of any meaningful endeavor. My journey began with an unmistakable nudge from God—a moment that stirred me from rest and urged me to step out in faith. That voice led me to take a bold leap, using my 401(k) savings to pursue a dream: *SchoolBanks, Inc.* SchoolBanks started as a side project to help a friend, more of a passive income stream than a company. I sold it through an LLC but never planned for real growth. Hold on to that thought—there's more to unpack later. Let's return to the pivotal moment of hearing God's voice.

That step of faith came with enthusiasm but lacked a full understanding of how to balance divine purpose with practical strategy. And that, as you'll see, is where things got complicated.

Proverbs 3:5-6 (TPT): *"Trust in the Lord completely, and do not rely on your own opinions. With all your heart rely on Him to guide you, and He will lead you in every decision you make."*

The chapters ahead are a candid look at entrepreneurship's ups and downs—preparation, hiring the right people, and listening to customers. I'll take you through moments of panic and peace, sharing how I found my footing when everything seemed lost.

This isn't a tale of overnight success but one of perseverance—learning to lean on faith while building with wisdom and planning. My goal is to inspire you to pursue your dreams with courage, clarity, and foresight.

Philippians 4:13 (AMP): *"I can do all things [which He has called me to do] through Him who strengthens and empowers me..."*

What makes this book unique isn't just my transparency but the deeper truths woven into each chapter. Failure doesn't have to define you—it can refine you if you're willing to face it, learn, and rise above it.

Whether you're new to entrepreneurship or have been navigating its twists for years, I hope my journey reminds you that setbacks aren't the end. They're setups for comebacks—opportunities to grow, reshape your character, and deepen your resolve.

James 1:2-4 (MSG): *"Consider it a sheer gift, friends, when tests and challenges come at you from all sides. You know that under pressure, your faith-life is forced into the open and shows its true colors."*

May this book guide those embarking on their own journey. Lord, let it comfort the weary, inspire dreamers, and remind us that trials have purpose. Teach us to embrace every step—whether stumbling or striding forward—knowing You are shaping us for greater things.

David A. Greene Jr.

Contents

ACKNOWLEDGMENTS   vii

Chapter 1 Introduction - My Journey from $100K to $0   2

Chapter 2 Hearing the Call - Spiritual Insights and Decision-
Making   7

Chapter 3 The Financial Gamble - Lessons in Stewardship 13

Chapter 4 Building the Right Team - People, Purpose, and
Potential   20

Chapter 5 Navigating Challenges - Resilience in the Face of
Adversity   27

Chapter 6 The Role of Faith - Trusting the Bigger Picture 34

Chapter 7 Redefining Success - Beyond Financial Gains   40

Chapter 8 The Power of Reflection - Learning from the
Journey   46

Chapter 9 Legacy and Impact - Building Beyond Yourself 53

Chapter 10 Closing Thoughts - The Journey Continues   58

ABOUT THE AUTHOR   62

ACKNOWLEDGMENTS

First and foremost, I want to thank God for seeing me
through this journey. Your guidance and grace have been my
anchor in every season.

To my wife, Katika, your constant support, encouragement,
and belief in me have been my greatest blessings. Thank you
for being my rock and my partner through it all.

Kids – Haley, Brian, Matthew – Love y'all to pieces!

To my siblings, Dee, LeVar, Lacey (Twin), thank you for
always having my back. Your love and encouragement
remind me of the strength of family.

To my parents, David Sr. (Big Greene), (Queen) Esther,
thank you for teaching me that I can achieve anything. Your
lessons and unwavering belief in me laid the foundation for
everything I am.

To my friends, ALL OF YOU 305+, thank you for being
exactly where I needed you when I needed you. Your
presence has been a source of strength and inspiration.
This book would not have been possible without each of
you. Thank you for being part of this journey and for
contributing to the story of my life.

"Buckle Up."

Chapter 1
Introduction - My Journey from $100K to $0

Entrepreneurship is often portrayed as the ultimate path to freedom, wealth, and purpose. But for me, the reality was far more nuanced—a rollercoaster of highs, lows, and some hard-earned lessons. My journey, which started with a voice, a vision, and $100,000 in savings, quickly spiraled into challenges I never saw coming. This chapter is my attempt to walk you through the beginnings of that journey, not as a cautionary tale, but as a guide to help you avoid the same pitfalls and, perhaps, to find strength in your own story.

The Start of the Dream

The idea of taking a leap of faith wasn't new to me. I've always believed that God's plans are bigger than ours, and when I felt led to reignite SchoolBanks, Inc., I knew I had to trust the visioning. Using $100,000 from my 401(k) to fund the dream seemed bold, even risky, but at the time, it felt necessary. Let me pause here and thank my lovely wife AGAIN for believing in God through me. Without her unwavering faith, this journey might have ended before it began. Together, we envisioned a thriving business that would serve a purpose and create generational impact.

But here's the thing about visions: they require not just faith but also preparation. I had one half of the equation—faith in abundance—but I lacked the foresight and planning to back it up. And that's where things got tricky. Imagine landing your dream job as a partner in a law firm, but you haven't even taken Legal 101. My excitement blinded me to the reality that success requires more than just passion; it requires a roadmap.

Jumping In Without a Plan

One of the earliest mistakes I made was diving in without a detailed, actionable roadmap. I was so eager to bring my vision to life that I bypassed essential steps like building a robust business plan. My enthusiasm led me to hire quickly, spend recklessly, and trust that my passion alone would carry the day. Look, I had a "plan," but it wasn't the right plan. And having the wrong plan is equivalent to having no plan at all.

What I learned—through hard and painful lessons—is that passion without a plan is like setting sail without a map. The wind might carry you forward, but without direction, you risk drifting aimlessly or running aground. My journey from $100,000 to $0 was marked by these kinds of missteps. Each one taught me a critical lesson about preparation and the price of overlooking the basics.

The Reality Check

The financial reality hit hard. Relying solely on my 401(k) savings put immense pressure on the business to succeed quickly. Entrepreneurship is rarely a sprint; it's a marathon. My single-source funding approach left no room for flexibility or unexpected costs, and the strain began to show almost immediately. I underestimated expenses and overestimated revenue—a combination that spelled disaster. This also pointed back to the lack of having the "right plan." Without it, money was spent on the wrong things, often. That spending led to even more unexpected costs and put more strain on the budget than I could overcome.

The People Puzzle

Another lesson came in the form of hiring. I made the mistake of building a team based on personalities and personal relationships rather than skills and the specific needs of the business. I wanted harmony. I wanted to be liked. I wanted to give back to my community. But what I needed was capability.

3

What I needed was skill. What I needed was experience. And, most importantly, what I needed was an actual plan for hiring. Yes, there's that word "plan" again.

As challenges mounted, I found myself stepping in to fix problems that a more skilled team could have handled. And if I'm being completely honest, I wasn't even skilled enough to fix some of the problems I was trying to address. It was a costly oversight, one that drained resources, time, and energy. But it also taught me an invaluable lesson: to prioritize expertise and strategic hiring over good intentions.

Hiring isn't just about filling roles; it's about building a foundation. And without the right foundation, the structure—no matter how promising—will eventually crumble.

Embracing the Lessons

Every setback was painful, but each one offered a chance to grow. I began to understand the importance of blending vision with practicality, balancing faith with planning, and seeking counsel from those who had walked similar paths. The journey was humbling, but it laid the groundwork for resilience and wisdom that I carry with me today.

If there's one takeaway I want to leave you with, it's this: Your dreams are worth pursuing, but they demand more than hope. They require strategy, humility, and the courage to learn from mistakes. As you read this book, I hope you'll find the tools and inspiration to navigate your own journey—with fewer bumps in the road and greater clarity along the way.

Practical Activities:
1. **Seek Mentorship and Counsel**
   Surround yourself with experienced advisors, mentors, or business coaches. Learn from their successes and mistakes to make informed decisions and avoid unnecessary pitfalls.

Spiritual (Bible-Based) Activities:
1. **Pray for Wisdom and Guidance**
   Reflect on **Proverbs 16:3**: "Commit to the Lord whatever you do, and he will establish your plans." Begin each day by praying for clarity, wisdom, and the courage to follow God's direction in your business decisions.
2. **Study and Apply Biblical Principles on Stewardship**
   Meditate on **Luke 14:28-30**, which emphasizes counting the cost before starting a project. Practice good stewardship by managing resources wisely and avoiding impulsive decisions that lead to unnecessary risks.

"Faith must be the fuel, but strategy must be the vehicle."

Chapter 2
Hearing the Call - Spiritual Insights and Decision-Making

It was one of the best nights of sleep I'd had in a long time. Newly married, with life feeling secure and full of promise, I rested deeply. Then it happened. God woke me up, and what I heard was crystal clear and life-changing: "Your 401(k) isn't meant for retirement; its purpose is to fund it."

In that moment, I believed wholeheartedly that this was my moment, my time to shine, my time to make millions, my divine assignment to reignite SchoolBanks, Inc. The vision was vivid and filled me with an undeniable sense of purpose. Excitement surged through me—it felt like confirmation that this was my moment to shine, to create something impactful, and yes, to make millions. Yet, as I've since learned, even the clearest spiritual insights need to be paired with discernment and preparation.

Jeremiah 29:11 (NIV): "For I know the plans I have for you,' declares the Lord, 'plans to prosper you and not to harm you, plans to give you hope and a future.'"

If you ever find yourself at a point in your journey where it feels like the only direction left is up, let me remind you: "Up" is a destination for you, but it's not yours to control. The Lord knows the plans, orchestrates the timing, and guides the steps. Pray—and then pray again—for understanding and direction to align with His plan, not just your desires.

Balancing Faith and Strategy

Spiritual insights are a gift—they provide clarity and direction in times of uncertainty. But they are not a substitute for strategy. Faith and practicality are not opposites; they are partners in the journey. Perhaps the real quote isn't "the circle of life is spiritual + practical," but for now, let's go with it.

One of my earliest mistakes was assuming that the vision was an automatic guarantee of success. I acted on it almost immediately, convinced that the clarity of God's call was all I needed. What I didn't do was pause long enough to ask, "How?" What steps should I take? Who should I consult? How could I align my faith with wisdom and practicality?

This gap between vision and execution created cracks that widened as time went on. Faith had to be the fuel, but strategy needed to be the vehicle. Without a detailed plan, I was like a race car driver charging toward a finish line without knowing the layout of the track. The Indy 500 is not the Monaco Grand Prix, and if you don't know the turns, you're bound to spin out or end up off course.

Seeking Counsel

One of the most valuable lessons I've learned is the importance of surrounding yourself with wise advisors. God often speaks through the people around us, but I was so focused on what I thought I knew that I didn't take the time to seek advice. My reality was, "Hey, I'm a former D1 football player and a successful IT professional—I know what I'm doing here." The actual reality? Pride was whispering that I had it all figured out, but it was the low valleys (aka failures) that eventually taught me to listen.

Proverbs 15:22 (TPT): "Your plans will fall apart right in front of you if you fail to get good advice. But if you first seek out multiple counselors, you'll watch your plans succeed."

Looking back, I wish I had consulted mentors, sought out experts in the field, and prayed for God to reveal the right people to guide me. Their insights wouldn't have replaced the vision, but they could have strengthened it—grounding my faith with practical steps.

The Cost of Acting in Isolation

Going it alone was costly. Without a sounding board, I made decisions based on emotion and assumptions rather than informed insight. This led to missteps that drained resources, time, and energy. Acting in isolation didn't just impact the business—it impacted me. I felt overwhelmed, frustrated, and, at times, completely lost. I wasn't ready to wave the white flag, but I was definitely searching for it.

If you're feeling that way right now, don't be discouraged. Go back to *Jeremiah 29:11*. Read it over and over until it settles in your heart. God's promise isn't to spare us from challenges but to prosper us through them.

A Lesson in Alignment

Over time, I began to see my journey not as a series of failures but as a process of alignment. Aligning spiritual conviction with practical execution became my north star. It wasn't enough to trust in the vision—I had to trust in the process of planning, preparation, and seeking help. This alignment transformed the way I approached challenges, teaching me that true success is found at the intersection of faith and wisdom.

And here's a truth that may surprise you: the success we often chase isn't the same as true success. True success isn't just about hitting financial goals or milestones; it's about living in alignment with your purpose and creating a lasting impact.

If there's one message I hope you take from this chapter, it's this: Never let pride, ego, or fear keep you from seeking guidance. Your vision is a seed, but it needs the soil of preparation, the water of counsel, and the sunlight of faith to grow. Trust the process, even when it feels slow or uncertain. God's timing is perfect, and His plans are greater than we can imagine.

Practical Activities:
1. **Document the Vision in Detail**
   After receiving a vision or idea, write it down in as much detail as possible. Break it into actionable steps and timelines, allowing you to translate inspiration into a clear roadmap. Regularly revisit this document to stay aligned with your goals.
2. **Conduct a Feasibility Analysis**
   Before acting on the vision, evaluate its practicality. Research your market, potential competitors, and customer needs. Use tools like SWOT analysis (Strengths, Weaknesses, Opportunities, Threats) to assess whether the vision is viable and identify areas requiring adjustment.
3. **Create a Decision-Making Framework**
   Establish a framework for making decisions that includes prayer, counsel, and data-driven analysis. Ensure that every decision aligns with both your vision and measurable outcomes. This will help balance faith with logical execution.
4. **Build a Support Network**
   Intentionally surround yourself with experienced advisors, mentors, and peers who can provide insight and hold you accountable. Actively engage with them by sharing your plans, challenges, and progress for feedback.

Spiritual (Bible-Based) Activities:
1. **Practice Spiritual Discernment**
   Reflect on **Proverbs 3:5-6**: "Trust in the Lord with all your heart and lean not on your own understanding; in all your ways submit to him, and he will make your paths straight." Pray for discernment before taking action and ask God to reveal His timing and strategy for the vision.
2. **Seek Godly Counsel Regularly**
   Live out **Proverbs 15:22**: "Plans fail for lack of counsel, but with many advisers they succeed."

Schedule regular meetings with spiritual mentors or trusted leaders to ensure your plans align with God's Word and will. Their wisdom can offer guidance you might not see on your own.

"Every dollar spent needs to align with the overall strategy and purpose of the business—it's not just about boldness, but balance."

Chapter 3
The Financial Gamble - Lessons in Stewardship

When I withdrew $100,000 from my 401(k), I did so with a heart full of hope and a head full of ambition. Using a 401(k) to kickstart a business isn't inherently a bad decision. If you're reading this, let me emphasize that point: funding a business through a 401(k) or any other financial injection can be a wise move when done strategically. But as with any financial choice, you want to position yourself to maximize the return. Now, let's return to my story.

At the time, withdrawing the money felt like an act of faith, a bold step toward building a legacy. What I didn't fully grasp was that even bold steps require careful calculation. The money I intended to use as a launching pad became a source of pressure and, eventually, a humbling lesson in the importance of stewardship.

Luke 14:28-30 (NLT): "But don't begin until you count the cost. For who would begin construction of a building without first calculating the cost to see if there is enough money to finish it? Otherwise, you might complete only the foundation before running out of money, and then everyone would laugh at you. They would say, 'There's the person who started that building and couldn't afford to finish it!'"

The Pressure of Self-Funding

Relying entirely on my 401(k) to fund the business wasn't just a financial decision—it was an emotional one. I saw the money as a tangible representation of my faith and commitment to the vision. But as the months went on and expenses piled up, I began to feel the weight of that choice. Every dollar spent became a reminder of how much I had on the line, and the pressure to succeed mounted with each passing day.

This approach left no room for error. Without additional funding sources or a financial safety net, any misstep threatened to derail the entire operation. Of course, I'd love to tell you I had a sound plan in place for how best to use the funding, but the truth is, I didn't. I underestimated how quickly the funds would dwindle and overestimated how soon the business would generate revenue. It was a recipe for stress, and it taught me that financial stewardship isn't just about boldness—it's about balance. Proper financial planning requires both accurate expense estimates and sound, data-backed revenue projections.

The Importance of Diversified Funding

If I could go back, I would have approached funding differently. Diversifying my financial resources would have given me the flexibility to navigate challenges without the constant fear of running out of money. Loans, grants, partnerships, and even crowdfunding could have supplemented my initial investment, reducing the burden on my personal savings.

Another viable option might have been to keep working my full-time job while laying the groundwork for the business. In this case, I still could have used a 401(k) rollover, but transitioning to a job that required less of my focus could have freed up time to develop the business without the overwhelming financial strain.

Proverbs 21:5 (MSG): "Careful planning puts you ahead in the long run; hurry and scurry puts you further behind."

Looking for alternative funding doesn't diminish faith—it enhances it by pairing belief with action. Faith isn't about doing everything on your own; it's about trusting that God provides multiple avenues for success. By exploring diverse financial options, I could have positioned myself to better weather the inevitable ups and downs of entrepreneurship.

Learning to Budget Wisely

Another critical lesson was the necessity of realistic budgeting. My initial budget, looking back, was based more on hope than on hard data. And let me tell you, looking at those numbers today makes me cringe. What was I thinking? But if you find yourself in a similar situation, don't throw in the towel. Adjust your approach, learn from the missteps, and keep moving forward.

Proper budgeting requires digging deep into the details—identifying potential costs, estimating realistic revenues, and building in a buffer for the unexpected. This would have been the perfect opportunity to consult mentors and industry experts, especially those familiar with the K-12 market, to ensure my numbers were grounded in reality.

Every dollar spent needs a purpose, a clear job that aligns with your overall strategy and contributes to the business's growth. Think of each dollar as a little employee whose job is to return with some friends. ☺ Each dollar should multiply its value through careful, intentional spending.

The Spiritual Side of Stewardship

Throughout this experience, I came to realize that stewardship isn't just about finances—it's a spiritual principle. God calls us to be faithful with what we've been given, whether it's money, time, or talents. Mismanaging resources isn't just a financial mistake; it's a missed opportunity to honor God with the gifts entrusted to us.

Matthew 25:21 (NIV): "His master replied, 'Well done, good and faithful servant! You have been faithful with a few things; I will put you in charge of many things. Come and share your master's happiness!'"

This verse became a guide for me in approaching every financial decision with prayer and intentionality. Stewardship is about aligning our resources with God's purpose, trusting that He will multiply what we manage wisely. It's not always easy, but it's a discipline that builds character and fosters long-term success.

Moving Forward with Lessons Learned

By the end of this chapter in my journey, I had gained a

new perspective on finances and faith. I learned to value preparation as much as passion, to seek counsel as much as courage, and to trust that even when resources seem scarce, God's provision is abundant.

If you're considering a similar leap of faith, my advice is simple: Do it with open eyes and a prepared heart. Take the time to plan, explore diverse resources, and treat every dollar with the care of a steward. Entrepreneurship is a calling, but it's also a responsibility—one that requires both boldness and wisdom.

As I reflect on this chapter of my life, I am grateful for the lessons it taught me. Stewardship, I now know, is a journey of faith and growth. It shapes not only our businesses but also our hearts. Let this serve as a reminder that even the hardest financial lessons can lead to the greatest spiritual growth.

Practical Activities:
1. **Develop a Multi-Source Funding Strategy**
   Explore diverse funding options beyond personal savings, such as small business loans, grants, partnerships, or crowdfunding. This diversification reduces financial strain and provides flexibility to navigate challenges without risking your personal finances entirely.
2. **Build a Contingency Fund**
   Allocate a percentage of your budget to an emergency or contingency fund. This buffer will help you manage unexpected costs, such as delayed revenue, increased expenses, or market fluctuations, without derailing your business.
3. **Create a Data-Driven Budget**
   Use real-world data and industry benchmarks to create a detailed and realistic budget. Break it down into specific categories (marketing, operations, salaries, etc.) and ensure every dollar spent is purpose-driven. Revisit and adjust this budget monthly based on actual performance.
4. **Pilot Your Business Concept**
   Before fully committing your resources, run a small-scale pilot to test your concept. Use this opportunity to gather customer feedback, refine your offering, and validate revenue assumptions, minimizing the risk of large-scale financial missteps.

Spiritual (Bible-Based) Activities:
1. **Pray for Wisdom in Stewardship**
   Reflect on **Proverbs 21:20**: "The wise store up choice food and olive oil, but fools gulp theirs down." Pray for discernment to manage your resources wisely, resisting the urge to spend impulsively and ensuring that every decision aligns with God's purpose.
2. **Commit Financial Decisions to God**
   Practice **Matthew 6:33**: "But seek first his kingdom

and his righteousness, and all these things will be given to you as well." Begin each financial planning session with prayer, asking for God's guidance to align your business goals with His kingdom priorities.

"No vision, no matter how strong, can succeed without capable hands and aligned hearts to bring it to life."

Chapter 4
Building the Right Team - People, Purpose, and Potential

As the business began to take shape, I realized something critical: no vision, no matter how strong, can succeed without the right people to bring it to life. To be clear, I did have a mission and vision statement. What I lacked, however, was a clear vision for the various aspects of a successful business—and more specifically, a K-12 business. You need a blueprint that anyone can review and follow while operating effectively in their respective roles. This chapter is about the power of teamwork, the importance of aligning values, and the lessons I learned—sometimes the hard way—about building a team that embodies both purpose and potential.

Proverbs 27:17 (AMP): "As iron sharpens iron, So one man sharpens [and influences] another [through discussion]."

The Hiring Mistakes

In the early days, my approach to hiring was driven more by urgency and familiarity than by strategy. I brought people on board quickly, often because I knew them, eager to fill roles and get the business moving. What I didn't fully consider were the long-term implications of those choices. The result was a team that, while well-meaning, wasn't always equipped to handle the demands of a growing company.

Let me be clear—this isn't about bashing the people I hired. They were, and still are, incredible individuals who have gone on to thrive in their respective careers. But hiring a "car salesperson of the year" to edit a blockbuster film would likely not lead to a box office success, no matter how talented they are in their field. Similarly, I learned that hiring without alignment to the role's requirements creates inefficiencies.

One of the biggest mistakes I made was prioritizing familiarity and likability over capability. I wanted to work with people I knew and enjoyed being around, but that didn't always translate to the skills and expertise the business needed. As challenges arose, gaps in experience and knowledge became glaringly obvious, and I found myself stepping in to fill those gaps instead of focusing on my role as a leader. Wearing multiple hats may be possible, but it's rarely the most effective way to grow a business.

Aligning Values and Vision

Through trial and error, I learned that successful teams are built on shared values and a clear understanding of the vision. It wasn't enough for someone to be talented; they also needed to believe in the mission of the business and commit to its success. Alignment between personal values and organizational goals created a sense of unity and purpose that made all the difference.

I remember hiring an exceptionally talented developer. His technical skills were unmatched, but he never truly bought into the vision of the company. In hindsight, I realized that this disconnect wasn't his fault—I hadn't clearly defined the vision or given him the opportunity to align with it. While his work was solid, it often missed the mark because I failed to provide a clear point of focus. That's on me, not him.

Amos 3:3 (NCV): "Two people will not walk together unless they have agreed to do so."

Once I began focusing on value alignment, the dynamic of the team shifted. I started looking for people who brought not only skills but also passion, integrity, and a willingness to grow. These qualities created a culture of collaboration and mutual respect that strengthened the business from the inside out. Interestingly, many of these new hires were college interns— hungry for growth and eager to contribute meaningfully.

21

The Importance of Diversity

Another invaluable lesson was the power of diversity—not just in terms of backgrounds but also in thought, experience, and perspective. A diverse team brought fresh ideas, challenged assumptions, and fostered innovation. It taught me to embrace different viewpoints and recognize the strength that comes from varied experiences. When I no longer had the funding to hire exactly what I needed, I had to find people who naturally aligned with where we were headed and could grow alongside the business.

1 Corinthians 12:12 (TPT): "Just as the human body is one, though it has many parts that together form one body, so too is Christ."

Investing in People

Building a strong team wasn't just about hiring the right people—it was about investing in them. Providing opportunities for growth, offering constructive feedback, and creating an environment where people felt valued were all critical to retaining top talent. I learned that leadership isn't about control; it's about empowerment.

When I started to view my role as a leader through the lens of service—helping my team succeed rather than directing their every move—the results were transformative. People flourished, ideas flowed, and the business became more resilient. If you've never read *The Mentor Leader* by Tony Dungy, I highly recommend it. It completely reshaped how I approached leadership and team development.

Letting Go When Necessary

Perhaps one of the hardest parts of leadership was recognizing when it was time to let someone go. Whether due to a lack of fit, performance issues, or shifting business needs, these decisions were never easy. But I came to understand that holding onto someone who isn't aligned with the mission can be more damaging than letting them go.

Each time I had to make that decision, I approached it with prayer and a commitment to handle the situation with grace and respect. Letting someone go wasn't a failure—it was an opportunity for both the individual and the organization to move forward in a way that better served everyone involved.

Moving Forward

The journey of building a team taught me that leadership is both an art and a science. It requires discernment, humility, and a willingness to adapt. As I look back, I'm grateful for the lessons learned and for the people who helped shape the business into what it became. My prayer is that every individual who touched SchoolBanks, no matter how briefly, continues to thrive, grow, and carry forward the lessons we learned together.

If you're building a team, my advice is this: Take your time. Look beyond resumes and focus on character, values, and potential. Invest in your people, create a culture of trust and collaboration, and never underestimate the power of diversity. A strong team is the foundation of a successful business, and the effort you put into building it will always be worth it.

Practical Activities:
1. **Develop Role-Specific Hiring Criteria**
   Define the skills, experience, and qualities needed for each role before starting the hiring process. Use these criteria to evaluate candidates objectively, ensuring alignment with the position's demands rather than relying on familiarity or urgency.
2. **Create a Comprehensive Onboarding Process**
   Design an onboarding program that clearly communicates the company's mission, vision, and values. Include role-specific training to set new hires up for success and ensure they understand their contributions to the larger goals.
3. **Foster a Culture of Feedback and Growth**
   Implement regular one-on-one meetings with team members to discuss their performance, provide constructive feedback, and identify growth opportunities. Use this time to reinforce their alignment with the mission and values of the organization.
4. **Encourage Cross-Functional Collaboration**
   Build opportunities for team members from diverse roles and backgrounds to work together on projects. This fosters innovation, strengthens relationships, and allows the team to leverage each other's unique strengths.

Spiritual (Bible-Based) Activities:
1. **Pray for Wisdom in Hiring and Leadership**
   Reflect on **James 1:5**: "If any of you lacks wisdom, you should ask God, who gives generously to all without finding fault, and it will be given to you." Pray for discernment in selecting the right team members and for guidance in leading them effectively.
2. **Practice Servant Leadership**
   Embrace the principle of **Mark 10:45**: "For even the Son of Man did not come to be served, but to serve,

and to give his life as a ransom for many." Approach leadership as an opportunity to serve and uplift your team, focusing on their success and well-being as the foundation of the business's growth.

"Resilience isn't about avoiding storms; it's about learning to dance in the rain and rebuild stronger after each one."

Chapter 5
Navigating Challenges - Resilience in the Face of Adversity

Every entrepreneurial journey comes with its share of challenges, and mine was no exception. The obstacles I faced tested my resolve, my faith, and my ability to adapt under pressure. This chapter is about those defining moments—the times when giving up seemed like the easiest option, but resilience kept me moving forward. Or did it? Could it be that I was too stubborn to see the signs that could have helped me avoid some of these challenges? Could I have prevented them altogether? Let's dig in and find out.

James 1:2-3 (AMP): "Consider it nothing but joy, my brothers and sisters, whenever you fall into various trials. Be assured that the testing of your faith [through experience] produces endurance [leading to spiritual maturity, and inner peace]."

The Unexpected Setbacks

No matter how prepared you think you are, some challenges catch you completely off guard. For me, one of the toughest moments came when a key client suddenly terminated their subscription. It wasn't just the financial blow—though that was painful—it was the emotional toll of feeling like I had failed to deliver. That client had been with us for years, and yet, in what felt like an instant, they were gone.

I remember sitting in my home office, staring at the email notification and feeling my stomach sink. Doubt hit me like a tidal wave. Was I cut out for this? Did I make a mistake pursuing this dream? Did I hear God's voice wrong?

In those moments, it was tempting to spiral into negativity, to feel sorry for myself, and to let failure win. But I learned something powerful: resilience begins with a shift in perspective. Instead of letting that setback define me, I chose to look for the lesson. I asked myself hard questions: *What can I learn from this experience? What processes need improvement? How can I serve my clients better moving forward?* That mindset shift turned the pain into purpose, and the loss became the foundation for growth.

Building a Support Network

One of the most valuable lessons I learned during this period was the importance of having a support network. Entrepreneurship can feel incredibly isolating, especially when things aren't going well. It's easy to feel like you're carrying the weight of the world on your shoulders. But I realized that leaning on others—whether friends, mentors, or fellow business owners—wasn't a weakness; it was a lifeline.

I started by reaching out to trusted friends from college and professional circles who believed in me and the vision for SchoolBanks. They weren't just cheerleaders—they were sounding boards, voices of reason, and, at times, sources of tough love. Over time, I was able to create a small advisory board for the business. This group, unlike friends or family, approached challenges with a mix of encouragement and strategic thinking because they were invested in the success of the business in a slightly different way. Their perspective was invaluable.

And let me say this: while social media groups can seem like an obvious solution for connection, not all of them deliver real value. Many are full of noise without much guidance. If you want genuine support, I suggest joining a local chamber of commerce or a professional group that meets regularly in person. There's something powerful about face-to-face connections that builds trust and fuels growth.

Adapting to Change

Challenges often require a willingness to adapt. I realized that clinging to familiar methods simply because they were comfortable was holding me back. Change can be uncomfortable, but it's often necessary for growth. I had to learn to pivot when circumstances demanded it and to approach problems with a mindset of innovation.

For instance, when the pandemic disrupted our operations, everything I knew about running SchoolBanks was suddenly upended. Instead of panicking (okay, maybe I panicked *a little*), I focused on rethinking how we delivered value. Virtual solutions, flexible service models, and innovative strategies became the new foundation. While the adjustment wasn't easy, embracing change ultimately made the business more resilient.

Isaiah 43:19 (TPT): "I am doing something brand new, something unheard of. Even now it sprouts and grows and matures. Don't you perceive it? I will make a way in the wilderness and open up flowing streams in the desert." — Even God embraces change.

The Power of Resilience

Resilience isn't just about surviving hardship; it's about emerging stronger on the other side. Each challenge I faced added to my capacity to handle future obstacles. It deepened my faith, strengthened my leadership, and taught me to find solutions even when the path wasn't clear.

One of my most defining moments of resilience came after months of rejections. I finally secured a new client, and the win felt monumental. It wasn't just about the financial relief—it was the affirmation that perseverance pays off.

But let's be real: sometimes resilience is built through humbling lessons. When I lost that first major client, I realized I needed to learn more about customer service—*real* customer service. I had gotten away with doing things casually when the business was a passive income stream. But now, as a full-time entrepreneur, I needed to sharpen my skills and take my commitment to the next level. Losing that client was painful, but it taught me lessons that positioned me to care for larger clients in the future.

Lessons Learned

As I reflect on the challenges I faced, several key lessons stand out:

1. **Embrace setbacks as opportunities for growth.**

Every challenge carries a lesson. Look for the wisdom it offers and use it to improve. In Genesis 50:20, Joseph's setbacks became the foundation for his leadership, and what others meant for harm, God used for good.

2. **Lean on your support network.** Don't try to navigate adversity alone. Surround yourself with people who uplift and challenge you. Even Moses needed Aaron to support him when he doubted his calling (Exodus 4:14-16).

3. **Stay open to change.** Adaptability is essential for survival. Sometimes, God uses disruption to point us toward better opportunities, like He did with Paul on the road to Damascus (Acts 9:3-6).

4. **Trust God's process.** Growth takes time. Trust that even when it's hard, God is working behind the scenes. Just as a seed takes time to grow, the results of your effort may not be immediate, but they are coming (Mark 4:26-29).

Moving Forward

Challenges are inevitable in entrepreneurship, but they don't have to define you. With resilience, faith, and a willingness to learn, you can turn even the most painful setbacks into powerful comebacks. Let this chapter serve as a reminder: adversity isn't the end—it's the beginning of something new.

Romans 8:28 (NIV): "And we know that in all things God works for the good of those who love him, who have been called according to his purpose."

Practical Activities:

1. **Perform a Post-Challenge Analysis**
   After encountering a setback, take the time to debrief and analyze what went wrong and why. Identify lessons learned and create an actionable plan to prevent similar issues in the future. Use this as a tool to strengthen your processes and decision-making.

2. **Diversify Your Client Base**
   This might be a stretch for a start-up, but if possible, avoid relying too heavily on a single client or revenue stream. Develop a client diversification strategy to spread risk and ensure that losing one account doesn't jeopardize your entire business.

3. **Establish a Contingency Playbook**
   Create a contingency plan for potential disruptions. Outline steps to handle various scenarios, such as a sudden client loss, economic downturns, or operational issues. Practice these scenarios with your team to ensure you're prepared to pivot when needed.

4. **Join a Peer Mastermind Group**
   Find a group of fellow entrepreneurs who meet regularly to share experiences, provide accountability, and exchange ideas. This kind of group fosters collaboration and offers fresh perspectives on challenges you may face.

Spiritual (Bible-Based) Activities:

1. **Reframe Setbacks with Faith**
   Meditate on **Romans 8:28**: "And we know that in all things God works for the good of those who love him, who have been called according to his purpose." Use setbacks as an opportunity to trust God's plan and seek His purpose in your challenges.

2. **Strengthen Your Faith Through Prayer and Gratitude**
   Reflect on **James 1:2-3**: "Consider it nothing but

joy, my brothers and sisters, whenever you fall into various trials..." Practice gratitude even in hard times by praying for wisdom and thanking God for the lessons embedded in your struggles.

"Surrender doesn't mean giving up; it means letting go of control and trusting God's timing and provision."

Chapter 6
The Role of Faith - Trusting the Bigger Picture

Faith has been my compass throughout this journey. In moments of uncertainty, doubt, or fear, it was my faith that reminded me of the bigger picture—of the purpose behind the challenges and the promise of better days ahead. This chapter is dedicated to exploring how faith not only sustains but also propels us forward, especially when the road is hard.

Hebrews 11:1 (NIV): "Now faith is confidence in what we hope for and assurance about what we do not see."

Stepping Out in Faith

From the very beginning, my entrepreneurial journey required an extraordinary leap of faith. Deciding to invest my life savings into a dream wasn't just a business decision; it was an act of trust—trust in God's plan, in the vision He placed on my heart, in my wife's belief that I wasn't just "playing games" about hearing from God, and in my ability to bring that vision to life. That last part, though—trusting in MY ability—was where I often went astray.

The truth is, gifts come from God. Knowledge can be acquired, but Godly wisdom is unique. When you tap into that wisdom, the knowledge you form carries you farther than you could ever go on your own strength. Stepping out in faith doesn't mean an absence of fear or doubt, nor does it diminish the gifts God has given you. It's about recognizing the source of those gifts and leaning into God's guidance.

I had plenty of doubts along the way. *What if I failed? What if I couldn't provide for my family?* These questions haunted me, but they also drove me to my knees in prayer. Faith gave me the courage to move forward despite the uncertainties, trusting that God's plans were bigger than my fears.

Proverbs 16:3 (TPT): "Before you do anything, put your trust totally in God and not in yourself. Then every plan you make will succeed."

Faith Through the Storms

The storms of life are inevitable, and as an entrepreneur, those storms often feel relentless. Financial struggles, client losses, and unforeseen challenges tested my faith repeatedly. I'm not saying this to discourage you, but the fact is, more businesses fail than succeed. There were countless moments when the weight of it all felt unbearable, and I questioned whether I had misunderstood God's calling. Believe me, I had my "Doubting Thomas" moments.

You may ask, *How do you doubt and then return to faith in the next breath?* Because that's what faith is—it's a muscle that gets stronger with exercise. At the start of my junior year in high school, I tried to bench 225 pounds and failed. By the time I was a senior in college, I could bench 365 pounds three times. Faith works the same way. By continuing to exercise it—even through failure—it grows stronger.

During these storms, I leaned on scripture, prayer, and the support of my church community to remind me of God's promises. Verses like *Jeremiah 29:11 (NIV): "For I know the plans I have for you," declares the Lord, "plans to prosper you and not to harm you, plans to give you hope and a future"* gave me the strength to persevere. These words reminded me that every storm serves a purpose, even when we can't see it at the time.

The Importance of Surrender

One of the hardest lessons I learned was the importance of surrender. As a former college football player, surrender wasn't part of my vocabulary. You're trained to fight through pressure and adversity, to never give up. But in business—and in faith—surrender doesn't mean giving up; it means letting go of control.

As a goal-oriented person, I wanted to dictate every

outcome, to ensure success through sheer determination. But faith required me to release that need for control and trust in God's timing and provision. Surrender meant being open to unexpected detours and trusting that they were part of the plan. It wasn't easy, but this shift in perspective brought a sense of peace and freedom I hadn't experienced before.

Psalm 37:5 (TPT): "Give God the right to direct your life, and as you trust him along the way, you'll find he pulled it off perfectly!"

Faith in Action

Faith isn't passive; it's active. It's not just about believing in God's promises but also about taking steps to align with them. For me, that meant showing up every day, even when I felt defeated. It meant putting in the work, seeking out opportunities, and continuing to dream big. Faith calls us to live with expectancy, waking up every day anticipating good things.

One way I put my faith into action was through service. Helping others—whether mentoring a young entrepreneur, volunteering at church, supporting my team, or writing this book—not only enriched their lives but also reignited my sense of purpose. Faith calls us to look beyond ourselves and contribute to something greater.

The Fruits of Faith

Over time, I began to see the fruits of faith. They didn't always come in the form of immediate success or tangible rewards. Sometimes, they came as lessons learned, relationships strengthened, or a deeper sense of resilience. Faith reshaped my perspective, allowing me to see the blessings even in the midst of struggle.

Romans 5:3-4 (NIV): "Not only so, but we also glory in our sufferings, because we know that suffering produces perseverance; perseverance, character; and character, hope."

A Lifelong Journey

Faith is not a destination; it's a journey. It's a daily choice to trust, to believe, and to move forward despite the unknowns. As I continue on this path, I carry with me the lessons faith has taught me—lessons of surrender, resilience, and the power of trusting in something greater than myself.

If there's one thing I hope you take away from this chapter, it's that faith is a powerful force. It doesn't eliminate challenges, but it gives us the strength to face them. It reminds us that we are not alone, that our struggles have purpose, and that brighter days are ahead.

Isaiah 40:31 (NIV): "But those who hope in the Lord will renew their strength. They will soar on wings like eagles; they will run and not grow weary, they will walk and not be faint."

Practical Activities:

1. **Build a Faith-Centered Morning Routine**
   Start each day with a routine that reinforces your faith, such as prayer, journaling about your goals, and reading scripture. A consistent routine helps you align your mindset with God's promises and approach challenges with a positive outlook.

2. **Identify and Track God's Provisions**
   Create a "faith journal" to document moments when God provided, even in small ways. Reviewing these entries during tough times can remind you of His faithfulness and renew your trust in His timing.

3. **Engage in Service to Strengthen Faith**
   Use your time, skills, or resources to serve others, whether through mentoring, volunteering, or supporting your community. Serving others fosters gratitude, builds resilience, and reminds you of the bigger purpose behind your work.

4. **Take Action Despite Uncertainty**
   Faith requires stepping out even when the outcome is unclear. Set one goal each week that challenges you to move forward despite fear or doubt, trusting that God is guiding your steps.

Spiritual (Bible-Based) Activities:

1. **Practice Surrender Daily**
   Reflect on **Psalm 37:5**: "Give God the right to direct your life, and as you trust him along the way, you'll find he pulled it off perfectly!" Write down areas of your business or life where you struggle to release control. Pray specifically for God's guidance and peace over these areas.

2. **Memorize and Meditate on Key Scriptures**
   Choose scriptures like **Isaiah 40:31** or **Hebrews 11:1** to memorize and meditate on during moments of doubt. Reciting these verses can help anchor your thoughts in faith when challenges arise.

"True success isn't about accumulation; it's about contribution and the legacy you leave behind."

Chapter 7
Redefining Success - Beyond Financial Gains

Success. For many of us, the word is synonymous with images of wealth, prestige, and influence. But my journey has taught me that true success isn't about any of those things. Cars, houses, money, fame—they're just things. They come and go. Sure, some of them are necessities in their own right, but they don't define success. And the lack of those things certainly doesn't mean failure.

This chapter is about redefining what success really means—looking beyond financial gains to focus on the deeper impact of our work, our relationships, and our personal growth. If you've read the Bible even a little, you've probably come across this verse: *"What good is it for someone to gain the whole world, yet forfeit their soul?" - Mark 8:36 (NIV)*. I won't preach to you about it here, but just trust me—it's true.

The Illusion of Success

When I first started, my definition of success was shaped by societal norms. I thought a thriving business, a growing bank account, and public recognition were the ultimate indicators of achievement. Don't get me wrong—a growing bank account is a *result* of success, but it's not the definition of it.

As I chased those goals, I realized they came at a cost. The long hours, the stress, and the constant pressure to "keep up" began to take a toll on my health, my relationships, and even my faith. It was a wake-up call. I had to ask myself, *Was I building a life of meaning, or was I just climbing a ladder that led nowhere?*

Reevaluating Priorities

The turning point came when I stopped focusing on *what* I wanted to achieve and started asking *why* I wanted to achieve it. I began asking myself deeper questions:

- What impact do I want to have?
- How do I want to be remembered?
- What legacy am I leaving for my family, my community, and the world?
- How am I impacting my employees, my customers, and the partners I work with?

This reevaluation of priorities led me to redefine success as something much more than financial gain. It became about creating value, fostering meaningful connections, and living in alignment with my purpose. Success was no longer a destination; it became a journey of continual growth and contribution.

Philippians 2:3-4 (ESV): "Do nothing from selfish ambition or conceit, but in humility count others more significant than yourselves. Let each of you look not only to his own interests, but also to the interests of others."

The Role of Relationships

One of the most profound lessons I learned was the importance of relationships. No amount of money or accolades can replace the joy of meaningful connections with family, friends, and colleagues. As I began to prioritize these relationships, I found they enriched my life in ways no material success ever could.

Building strong relationships required intentionality. It meant setting aside time for the people who mattered most, being present in the moment, and showing genuine care and appreciation. For example, in team meetings, I made it a point to really talk to my team. I got to know them. Did someone's kid make a big play in their big game? Were their parents coming into town? Maybe they needed a little extra time for family. What I learned about my team began to impact how I led them—and that made all the difference.

Making an Impact

Redefining success also meant focusing on the impact I could make. Whether through my business, community involvement, or personal interactions, I wanted my life to be a force for good. This shift in perspective transformed how I approached my work. It wasn't just about profits anymore—it was about purpose.

I started seeking out opportunities to give back, mentor others, and create solutions to real-world problems. If you've never volunteered with or hired interns from "Year Up," do yourself a favor: look it up and get involved. It's one of the most fulfilling things you can do. The sense of fulfillment I gained from making a positive impact far outweighed any financial reward.

Finding Balance

Redefining success also meant finding balance. Achieving great things professionally is meaningless if it comes at the expense of your well-being or your relationships. Balance required me to set boundaries, maintain a schedule, practice self-care, and prioritize my spiritual and emotional health.

Was balance always easy to maintain? Absolutely not. But it was essential. It reminded me that success is holistic—it encompasses every aspect of our lives, from our careers to our personal growth to our contributions to the world.

A New Definition of Success

Today, my definition of success looks very different from what it once was. Success, to me, is about living a life of purpose, integrity, and joy. It's about making a positive impact, building meaningful relationships, and staying true to my values. It's about finding contentment in the journey and trusting that God's plan is greater than any goal I could set for myself.

Moving Forward

If there's one thing I've learned, it's that success is deeply personal. It's not about living up to someone else's standards or chasing external validation. It's about aligning your life with your values, embracing your unique purpose, and finding joy in the journey.

As you reflect on your own definition of success, I encourage you to ask yourself:

- What truly matters to me?
- How can I use my gifts and resources to make a difference?
- What kind of legacy do I want to leave?

Success, I've come to realize, isn't about what we achieve—it's about who we become in the process. And that, more than anything, is worth striving for. It's about them, not about me. Go back and read *Philippians 2:3-4* again if you need a reminder.

Practical Activities:

1. **Define Your Personal Mission Statement**
   Take time to write a personal mission statement that outlines your values, purpose, and long-term vision for your life and business. This statement serves as a compass to guide decisions and ensure your efforts align with what truly matters.

2. **Create a Relationship-Building Plan**
   Dedicate intentional time to strengthen key relationships in your life. This can include scheduling regular family dinners, one-on-one meetings with team members, or community involvement. Build trust and connection by genuinely investing in others.

3. **Set Impact-Driven Goals**
   Develop business or personal goals that prioritize making a positive difference, such as mentoring a young entrepreneur, supporting a charitable cause, or creating products that address real-world challenges.

4. **Establish Work-Life Boundaries**
   Design a weekly schedule that includes work, personal time, and rest. Use tools like time-blocking or a digital calendar to ensure balance and accountability. This helps prevent burnout and ensures you're nurturing all areas of your life.

Spiritual (Bible-Based) Activities:

1. **Practice Humble Service**
   Reflect on **Philippians 2:3-4 (ESV):** "Do nothing from selfish ambition or conceit, but in humility count others more significant than yourselves. Let each of you look not only to his own interests, but also to the interests of others." Regularly ask yourself how your actions can serve and uplift others and look for opportunities to act selflessly.

"Reflection isn't about dwelling on the past; it's about using it as a compass to navigate the future with clarity."

Chapter 8
The Power of Reflection - Learning from the Journey

Life moves fast, and as entrepreneurs, it's easy to get caught up in the hustle and bustle of daily demands. But one of the most valuable practices I've embraced is the power of reflection. Taking time to pause, evaluate, and learn from the journey has been transformative—not only for my business but also for my personal growth.

The Need for Reflection

In the early days of my entrepreneurial journey, I rarely took time to reflect. I was so focused on the next task, the next goal, the next milestone that I overlooked the importance of stepping back to assess where I had been. Over time, I realized that without reflection, I was at risk of repeating mistakes, missing opportunities, and losing sight of my purpose.

Reflection is more than just looking back. It's about gaining insight, identifying patterns, and making intentional adjustments for the future. It's about asking the hard questions: *What worked? What didn't? How have I grown? What still needs work?* These questions became a cornerstone of my personal and professional development.

Reflecting also strengthens your faith muscles. When you can look back and see the track record of your results—and pinpoint where God's hand was at work—it builds a confidence that carries you forward. Faith isn't just about believing; it's about seeing God's track record, learning, and trusting more as you reflect on where you've been.

Learning from Mistakes

Mistakes are inevitable, but they are also some of our greatest teachers. Through reflection, I've been able to dissect my missteps and uncover valuable lessons. For example, I once pursued a major partnership opportunity without fully understanding the terms. The deal fell through, leaving me frustrated and taken advantage of, but by reflecting on the experience, I learned the importance of thorough preparation and clear communication.

Another mistake? Talking to a firm about a potential partnership without having an MNDA (Mutual Non-Disclosure Agreement) in place. Ouch. They took everything I shared and used it to enhance their solution, effectively cutting SchoolBanks out of some future opportunities. That one stung. But even in that, reflection showed me the lesson: Protect your ideas and always take the necessary precautions.

Reflection helped me reframe mistakes not as failures but as opportunities for growth. It allowed me to extract the wisdom from each experience and apply it moving forward. This shift in perspective made me a better leader, a better strategist, and, honestly, a better person.

Celebrating Wins

Reflection isn't just about analyzing challenges; it's also about celebrating successes. As entrepreneurs, we often move from one goal to the next without pausing to acknowledge our achievements. But taking time to celebrate wins, both big and small, is crucial for maintaining motivation and morale.

I've learned to reflect on what went well and why. *What strategies worked? What strengths did I leverage?* These insights not only reinforced positive behaviors but also boosted my confidence, resilience, and most importantly, a business that I was aligning with God's purpose. Celebrating wins reminded me of how far I had come and fueled my passion for the road ahead. Plus, let's be honest: Sometimes, you just need to pat yourself on the back for making it through the day.

Psalm 126:3 (NLT): " Yes, the LORD has done amazing things for us! What joy!"

The Practice of Journaling

One of the most effective tools for reflection has been journaling. Writing down my thoughts, experiences, and lessons has provided clarity and perspective. It's a space where I can process emotions, brainstorm ideas, and track my progress over time.

Journaling doesn't have to be elaborate. Sometimes, it's as simple as jotting down a few key takeaways from the day. Other times, it's a deep dive into a specific challenge or decision. Whatever the approach, the act of putting pen to paper (or fingers to keyboard) has been a powerful way to organize my thoughts and capture the essence of my journey. Fun fact: Journaling gave birth to this book.

Seeking Feedback

Reflection isn't always a solo activity. Seeking feedback from trusted mentors, colleagues, and friends has been invaluable. Remember what we talked about in Chapter's 2 and 4? You need a trustworthy sounding board—not just for laughs and encouragement but for real growth.

Feedback highlights blind spots I might have missed and offers insights I wouldn't have considered on my own. Most importantly, I go to God in prayer, asking Him to reveal the lessons I needed to learn, what I did well, and how well I honored Him in the process. Ultimately, all that we do should aim to first please God.

Approaching feedback with an open mind and a humble heart isn't always easy, but it's necessary for growth. Reflection, combined with external feedback, has helped me refine my strategies, improve my leadership, and deepen my relationships.

Moving Forward with Clarity

The power of reflection lies in its ability to illuminate the path forward. By taking time to learn from the past, I've been able to navigate the present with greater clarity and confidence. Reflection has become a regular practice—a habit that keeps me grounded, focused, and aligned with my purpose.

Philippians 3:12-16 (MSG): " I'm not saying that I have this all together, that I have it made. But I am well on my way, reaching out for Christ, who has so wondrously reached out for me. Friends, don't get me wrong: By no means do I count myself an expert in all of this, but I've got my eye on the goal, where God is beckoning us onward—to Jesus. I'm off and running, and I'm not turning back.

So let's keep focused on that goal, those of us who want everything God has for us. If any of you have something else in mind, something less than total commitment, God will clear your blurred vision—you'll see it yet! Now that we're on the right track, let's stay on it."

As you navigate your own journey, I encourage you to make time for reflection. Use it as a tool to learn, to grow, and to celebrate. Let it guide you toward your goals while keeping you anchored in your values. The journey of entrepreneurship is filled with lessons, and reflection ensures that none of them go to waste.

Moving forward, let reflection be part of your compass. It will not only show you where you've been but also light the way to where you're going.

Practical Activities:
1. **Schedule Regular Reflection Time**
   Set aside a dedicated time each week or month to reflect on your progress. Use prompts such as:
   o   What went well this week, and why?
   o   What challenges did I face, and how did I respond?
   o   What lessons can I take into the next week? This practice ensures you consistently learn from your experiences and refine your approach.
2. **Create a Wins and Lessons Log**
   Maintain a simple document or journal where you record both your wins and lessons learned. For each entry, include the key takeaway and an actionable step to reinforce or improve upon it.
3. **Seek Constructive Feedback Regularly**
   Identify a trusted group of mentors, peers, or colleagues who can provide honest feedback on your work or leadership style. Incorporate their insights into your reflections to uncover blind spots and areas for growth.
4. **Implement a Quarterly Review Process**
   Every quarter, perform a detailed review of your business and personal goals. Assess what's working, what's not, and how your efforts align with your long-term purpose. Use this time to celebrate successes and make strategic adjustments.

Spiritual (Bible-Based) Activities:
1. **Reflect on God's Faithfulness Through Scripture and Prayer**
   Meditate on **Psalm 126:3**: "Yes, the LORD has done amazing things for us! What joy!" Spend time thanking God for His guidance and identifying moments where His hand was at work in your journey. Let this reflection strengthen your faith for the future.

2. **Align Reflections with Your Spiritual Goals**
   Reflect on **Philippians 3:12-16** and ask yourself how your actions and decisions align with your ultimate purpose in Christ. Use this as a spiritual checkpoint to ensure your focus remains on honoring God and living out His calling.

"A meaningful legacy isn't just about what you leave behind—it's about the lives you impact along the way."

Chapter 9
Legacy and Impact - Building Beyond Yourself

Maybe you've heard of these terms—Godpreneurship and Kingdom Business Ownership. These are God-focused approaches to entrepreneurship that aren't just about creating a business; they're about creating a legacy. Before I go any further, let me give credit where it's due: I learned the term Godpreneur from Alex Miranda, a marketing guru and business coach, and Kingdom Business Owner (KBO) from Minister Kimberley Savage, the Purpose Central leader at Linked Up Church.

Now, back to it. As my journey progressed, I began to think more deeply about the impact I wanted to leave behind—on my family, my community, and the world—all while honoring God. This chapter is about the power of legacy and how building beyond yourself can bring lasting meaning to your work.

Proverbs 13:22 (TPT): "The benevolent man leaves an inheritance that endures to his children's children, but the wealth of the wicked is treasured up for the righteous."

The Shift to Legacy Thinking

In the early days of my entrepreneurial journey, my focus was largely on immediate goals—meeting deadlines, growing revenue, and achieving milestones. But as I gained experience, I started to ask bigger questions.

- *What am I building that will last?*

- *How will my work impact others long after I'm gone?*
- *Would it be enough to pay for my kids' college tuition or my great-great-grandkids' college tuition? What about beyond that?*

Legacy thinking shifted my perspective. It reminded me that success isn't just about what we achieve in the moment but about the foundation we lay for the future. It's about creating something that outlives us and continues to bring value to others.

Investing in People

One of the most meaningful ways to build a legacy is by investing in people. Whether through mentorship, leadership, or community engagement, empowering others to grow and succeed became a central focus of my work. I realized that the impact I could have on someone's life was far greater than any financial success.

I absolutely love a text chat I'm in where most of the people were once my team members. Now, I get to enjoy seeing their success in their respective walks. The best part? I get to hear their stories about mentoring others and paying it forward.

Mentoring young entrepreneurs, providing opportunities for my team, and supporting initiatives that uplift my community brought a sense of fulfillment that no amount of money could match. These investments in people created ripple effects that extended far beyond my immediate reach. Thinking beyond myself helped me see that even where I may have failed, I'm still able to help others avoid those same pitfalls.

Creating Sustainable Systems

Legacy also requires sustainability. It's not enough to build something great; it needs to be built to last. This meant creating systems and structures that could thrive without my constant involvement. It meant empowering others to take ownership and ensuring the business was adaptable to change. If 2020 taught us anything, it's that every business needs to be ready to deal with change.

Building sustainable systems took time and effort, but it was a critical step in creating a legacy. It allowed me to step back and focus on the bigger picture, knowing that what I had built was in capable hands. Creating those systems could be a whole book on its own. Depending on the year you're reading this, keep an eye out for that book—it might be coming in about 12 months after this one releases.

Leaving a Positive Impact

At the heart of legacy is impact. It's about using our resources, talents, and influence to make a difference in the lives of others. For me, this meant prioritizing social responsibility and aligning my business with causes I cared about. Whether it was supporting my local church, championing diversity in the corporate world, or giving back to underserved communities, making a positive impact has been a cornerstone of my legacy.

The Legacy of Faith

Faith played a significant role in shaping my approach to legacy. It reminded me that everything I have is a gift from God, entrusted to me to steward wisely. My faith encouraged me to think beyond myself and to use my work as a way to glorify God and serve others. Building a legacy rooted in faith ensured that my efforts would align with a purpose greater than myself.

Moving Forward with Purpose

As I reflect on the concept of legacy, I'm reminded that it's not about perfection; it's about intention. It's about making choices every day that align with your values and contribute to a greater good. Legacy isn't something you build overnight—it's the result of consistent, purposeful actions over time.

If there's one thing I hope you take away from this chapter, it's that building a legacy is within your reach. It's about looking beyond yourself, investing in others, and leaving the world better than you found it. As you navigate your own journey, I encourage you to think about the legacy you want to create and to take steps every day to make it a reality.

Hebrews 13:16 (TPT): "We will show mercy to the poor and not miss an opportunity to do acts of kindness for others, for these are the true sacrifices that delight God's heart."

Practical Activities:

1. **Create a Legacy Blueprint**
   Develop a detailed plan that outlines the impact you want to leave behind. Include specific goals for your family, community, and business. Identify actionable steps to work toward those goals, such as creating scholarship funds, mentoring young leaders, or supporting charitable initiatives.

2. **Establish a Mentorship Program**
   Set up a formal mentorship program within your business or community. Use your experiences to guide others, and empower them to build their own success. This investment in people fosters growth and ensures your impact extends beyond your immediate reach.

3. **Develop Sustainable Business Systems**
   Design processes and systems that allow your business to thrive without your direct involvement. Focus on succession planning, documenting workflows, and training team members to take on leadership roles to ensure your vision endures.

4. **Align Business Goals with Social Responsibility**
   Identify causes that align with your values and incorporate them into your business strategy. For example, dedicate a portion of profits to charitable organizations, partner with local nonprofits, or develop products that address societal needs.

Spiritual (Bible-Based) Activities:

1. **Live Out Acts of Kindness**
   Meditate on **Hebrews 13:16**: "We will show mercy to the poor and not miss an opportunity to do acts of kindness for others." Make intentional efforts to show kindness daily—whether through giving, volunteering, or simply offering encouragement to those around you.

"Success isn't the destination; it's the journey of becoming the best version of yourself while using your gifts to serve others."

Chapter 10
Closing Thoughts - The Journey Continues

As I bring this book to a close, I want to leave you with a final reflection: the journey of entrepreneurship, like life itself, is ever-evolving. It's a path filled with challenges, triumphs, lessons, and growth. And while this book captures my journey thus far, it's far from the end. The lessons I've shared—about faith, resilience, stewardship, leadership, and legacy—are not static. They continue to unfold and deepen as I navigate new seasons and opportunities. You can bet there will be a Part 2 to this book, just as there will be multiple parts to your successful journey.

The Ever-Evolving Journey

Entrepreneurship has been one of the greatest teachers of my life. Most importantly, it strengthened my relationship with God and reinforced my faith. It has taught me to embrace uncertainty, persevere through adversity, and find purpose even in the most unexpected places. Each challenge has been an opportunity to grow, and every success has been a reminder of the power of faith and hard work.

This journey has shown me that success is not the destination—it's the process. It's the courage to take the first step, the resilience to keep going, and the humility to learn along the way. Success is about becoming the best version of yourself and using your gifts to serve others. Yes, you're in business to make money—as you should and as you will. But the impact of serving someone well in your business pays off in more than just dollars and cents.

Final Lessons

As you reflect on your own path, I want to leave you with a few parting lessons:

1. **Define Success on Your Own Terms:** Don't let society dictate what success looks like for you. Align your goals with your values and measure your progress by the impact you make. Better yet, align your goals with your God-given purpose. And it's perfectly OK to include making money as part of your success. Just don't make it the greatest or only measure of success.

2. **Embrace the Power of Resilience:** Challenges will come, but they don't have to define you. Each setback is an opportunity to grow stronger, wiser, and more determined. Trust that God has given you everything you need to succeed, even if today doesn't look that way. Be prepared and open to pivoting as He leads you.

3. **Invest in Relationships:** The people you surround yourself with will shape your journey. Build meaningful connections, seek out mentors, and pour into others with generosity and intention. Picture your dinner table filled with these connections and mentors—what would that look like? Would you be sitting alone, or enjoying a masterful meal with solid individuals?

4. **Stay True to Your Purpose:** Let your purpose guide your decisions. When your work aligns with your calling, it becomes a source of joy and fulfillment. Don't discount the journey you'll take as you march toward your purpose. Who knew my failures and hard lessons in business would lead me to this purpose track? How do I know this purpose is for real? You— you're reading this book. You purchased this book. This book is a tool you can revert to for months and years to come, keeping you grounded while you soar!

5. **The Process of Trust:** Success takes time. Be patient with yourself, trust in the journey, and know that every step is part of a greater plan. For some, the process and journey look exactly as expected—like starting a car dealership and selling cars. For others, they start a K-12 tech company and end up writing a book! Hope that made you chuckle.

James 1:12 (TPT): "If your faith remains strong, even while surrounded by life's difficulties, you will continue to experience the untold blessings of God! True happiness comes as you pass the test with faith and receive the victorious crown of life promised to every lover of God!"

Gratitude for the Journey

Writing this book has been a deeply personal and reflective experience. It has given me the chance to look back on the lessons I've learned, the people who have shaped my journey, and my faith in God and salvation through Jesus Christ that have sustained me. I am profoundly grateful for the opportunity to share my story with you.

My hope is that these pages inspire you to pursue your dreams with courage and conviction. Whether you are just starting out or well along the way, know that your journey matters. The challenges you face, the victories you celebrate, and the impact you make are all part of a story that is uniquely yours.

As you continue on your journey, I invite you to stay connected. Share your thoughts, successes, and challenges with me. I believe in the power of community and the importance of supporting one another along the way. If this book has resonated with you, I'd love to hear your story.

I've created ways for us to stay connected and shared some helpful resources on my website, www.dgreenejr.com. Whether you have questions, reflections, or simply want to connect, I'd love to listen and encourage you as you take the next step in your journey.

Looking Ahead

While this book marks the end of one chapter, it also marks the beginning of the next. The journey continues, with new challenges to face, new lessons to learn, and new opportunities to embrace. I am excited for what lies ahead and grateful for the path that has brought me here.

The journey is yours to shape. Embrace it with faith, courage, and a heart full of gratitude. And remember: the best is yet to come!

Jeremiah 29:11 (TPT): "For I know the plans I have for you, says the Lord. They are plans for good and not for disaster, to give you a future filled with hope."

ABOUT THE AUTHOR

David A. Greene Jr. is a visionary entrepreneur, seasoned IT leader, and former Division 1 football athlete with a track record of transforming challenges into opportunities. With over two decades of experience in technology and leadership, he has built businesses that bridge innovation with real-world solutions. As the founder of **SchoolBanks, Inc.** and a partner at **7th Layer Tech**, David is driven by a passion for solving problems, empowering others, and leaving a lasting impact.

His journey—marked by bold leaps of faith, hard-earned wisdom, and relentless perseverance—has inspired countless individuals to step into their purpose with confidence. Beyond business, David is a devoted family man, a mentor to aspiring leaders, and a firm believer in the power of faith to shape success.

Through his work and writing, he aims to challenge conventional thinking, ignite ambition, and equip the next generation with the tools they need to thrive. Connect with him at **The100kCrashBook@gmail.com** to share your story, exchange ideas, or learn more about his mission.